Quotation Marks

Mary Elizabeth Salzmann

Published by SandCastle™, an imprint of ABDO Publishing Company, 4940 Viking Drive, Edina, Minnesota 55435.

Printed in the United States.

Photo credits: Eyewire Images, PhotoDisc

Library of Congress Cataloging-in-Publication Data

Salzmann, Mary Elizabeth, 1968-
  Quotation marks / Mary Elizabeth Salzmann.
    p. cm. -- (Punctuation)
  Includes index.
  ISBN 1-57765-624-5
    1. English language--Punctuation--Juvenile literature. 2. Quotation marks--Juvenile literature. [1. Quotation marks. 2. English language--Punctuation.] I. Title.

PE1450 .S267 2001
428.1--dc21
                                                                    2001033024

The SandCastle concept, content, and reading method have been reviewed and approved by a national advisory board including literacy specialists, librarians, elementary school teachers, early childhood education professionals, and parents.

Let Us Know

After reading the book, SandCastle would like you to tell us your stories about reading. What is your favorite page? Was there something hard that you needed help with? Share the ups and downs of learning to read. We want to hear from you! To get posted on the ABDO Publishing Company Web site, send us email at:

sandcastle@abdopub.com

About SandCastle™
Nonfiction books for the beginning reader

- Basic concepts of phonics are incorporated with integrated language methods of reading instruction. Most words are short, and phrases, letter sounds, and word sounds are repeated.

- Readability is determined by the number of words in each sentence, the number of characters in each word, and word lists based on curriculum frameworks.

- Full-color photography reinforces word meanings and concepts.

- "Words I Can Read" list at the end of each book teaches basic elements of grammar, helps the reader recognize the words in the text, and builds vocabulary.

- Reading levels are indicated by the number of flags on the castle.

Look for more SandCastle books in these three reading levels:

Level 1 (one flag)	Level 2 (two flags)	Level 3 (three flags)

Grades Pre-K to K 5 or fewer words per page	**Grades K to 1** 5 to 10 words per page	**Grades 1 to 2** 10 to 15 words per page

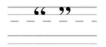

These are quotation marks.

I know when to use quotation marks.

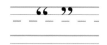

Quotation marks show that someone is speaking.

Olivia says, "Please push me on the swing."

Quotation marks go before and after a word or sentence.

My kitten says, "Meow."

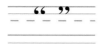

The first word inside quotation marks is usually capitalized.

Harry asks, "Can you hear me?"

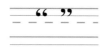

Valerie is writing a story.

It begins, "Once there was a monkey that loved bananas."

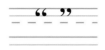

Names of nursery rhymes use **quotation marks**.

I can read "Ladybird" and "Three Little Kittens."

Song names go inside quotation marks.

Ling is playing "Heart and Soul" on the piano.

Use quotation marks around a word that is being defined.

Paul knows what "aboard" means.

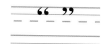

What does Nora say
when the doctor checks
her mouth?

("Aaah")

Words I Can Read

Nouns

A noun is a person, place, or thing

bananas (buh-NA-nuhz) p. 13

doctor (DOK-tur) p. 21

kitten (KIT-uhn) p. 9

monkey (MUHNG-kee) p. 13

mouth (MOUTH) p. 21

names (NAYMZ) pp. 15, 17

nursery rhymes (NUR-sur-ee RIMEZ) p. 15

piano (pee-AN-oh) p. 17

quotation marks (kwoh-TAY-shuhn MARKSS) pp. 5, 7, 9, 11, 15, 17, 19

sentence (SEN-tuhnss) p. 9

song (SAWNG) p. 17

story (STOR-ee) p. 13

swing (SWING) p. 7

word (WURD) pp. 9, 11, 19

Proper Nouns

A proper noun is the name of a person, place, or thing

Harry (HAIR-ee) p. 11

"Heart and Soul" (HART AND SOLE) p. 17

"Ladybird" (LAY-dee-burd) p. 15

Ling (LING) p. 17

Nora (NOR-uh) p. 21

Olivia (oh-LI-vee-uh) p. 7

Paul (PAWL) p. 19

"Three Little Kittens" (THREE LIT-uhl KIT-uhnz) p. 15

Valerie (VAL-uh-ree) p. 13

Pronouns

A pronoun is a word that replaces a noun

I (EYE) pp. 5, 15

it (IT) p. 13

me (MEE) pp. 7, 11

someone (SUHM-wuhn) p. 7

that (THAT) pp. 13, 19

there (THAIR) p. 13

these (THEEZ) p. 5

what (WUHT) pp. 19, 21

you (YOO) p. 11

Verbs

A verb is an action or being word

are (AR) p. 5
asks (ASKSS) p. 11
begins (bi-GINZ) p. 13
being (BEE-ing) p. 19
can (KAN) pp. 11, 15
checks (CHEKSS) p. 21
defined (di-FINED) p. 19
does (DUHZ) p. 21
go (GOH) pp. 9, 17

hear (HIHR) p. 11
is (IZ) pp. 7, 11, 13, 17, 19
know (NOH) p. 5
knows (NOHZ) p. 19
loved (LUHVD) p. 13
means (MEENZ) p. 19
playing (PLAY-ing) p. 17
push (PUSH) p. 7
read (REED) p. 15

say (SAY) p. 21
says (SEZ) pp. 7, 9
show (SHOH) p. 7
speaking (SPEEK-ing) p. 7
use (YOOZ) pp. 5, 15, 19
was (WUHZ) p. 13
writing (RITE-ing) p. 13

Adjectives

An adjective describes something

capitalized (KAP-uh-tuhl-eyezd) p. 11

first (FURST) p. 11
her (HUR) p. 21

my (MYE) p. 9

Adverbs

An adverb tells how, when, or where something happens

aboard (uh-BORD) p. 19
once (WUHNSS) p. 13

please (PLEEZ) p. 7

usually (YOO-zhoo-uhl-ee) p. 11

23

Glossary

aboard – on or in a boat, train, or airplane

bananas – long, curved, yellow fruits

capitalized – beginning with a capital letter or written in all capital letters

defined – described or explained something

nursery rhymes – poems written for young children

piano – a large keyboard instrument that makes musical sounds when hammers inside hit metal strings

usually – almost always